VERY LITTLE
IS NEEDAD
TO MAKE
A HAPPY LIFE,
IT IS ALL WITHIN
YOURSE LF, IN
YOUR WAY OF
THINKING

..................MARCUS AURELIUS..................

www.ingramcontent.com/pod-product-compliance
Lightning Source LLC
Chambersburg PA
CBHW070332190526
45169CB00005B/1864